FINDING
the Words to
PRAY

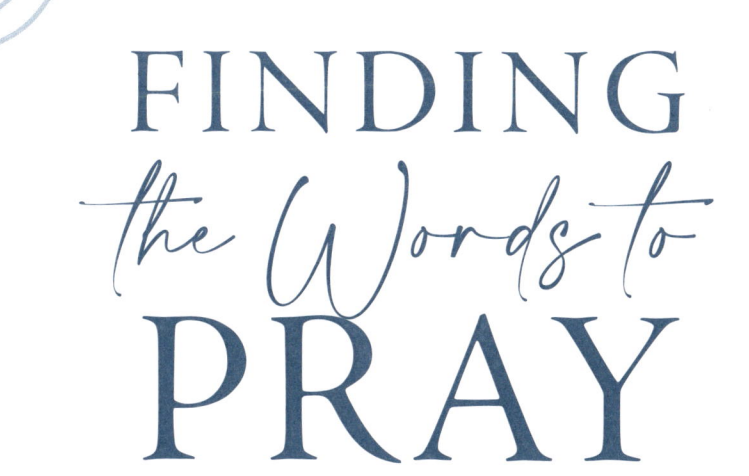

50 Scriptures to Guide Your Prayers

Introduction & Prayers from
Nancy DeMoss Wolgemuth

©2023 *Revive Our Hearts*

Published by *Revive Our Hearts*
P.O. Box 2000, Niles, MI 49120

ISBN: 978-1-959704-01-0

Printed in the United States of America.

All rights reserved. No part of this publication may be reproduced in any form without permission from the publisher, except in the case of brief quotations embodied in other works or reviews.

Edited by Erin Davis, Ashley Gibson, Mindy Kroesche, and Mindi Stearns.

Designed by Austin Collins.

Scripture quotations, unless otherwise indicated, are from the Christian Standard Bible, Copyright © 2017 by Holman Bible Publishers. Used by permission. Christian Standard Bible® and CSB® are federally registered trademarks of Holman Bible Publishers, all rights reserved.

CONTENTS

FROM NANCY'S HEART 4
PRAYERS FOR SEASONS OF WAITING 7
PRAYERS FOR WISDOM AND UNDERSTANDING 29
PRAYERS FOR TRANSFORMATION 51
PRAYERS FOR THE CHURCH 77
PRAYERS FOR PRODIGALS 95
PRAYERS FOR COMFORT 117
PRAYERS OF DESPERATION 139
PRAYERS OF REPENTANCE 161
PRAYERS FOR REVIVAL 187
PRAYERS OF PRAISE 211

FINDING THE WORDS TO PRAY

From Nancy's Heart

Do you ever wonder why it can be so difficult to pray? Prayer involves humbling ourselves, acknowledging that we're needy, and asking God to help us. That shouldn't be so hard, right? After all, we *are* needy.

Yet who among us doesn't struggle at times to find words for our prayers? Whether asking God for provision to pay this month's bills or praying for a prodigal child or interceding for a nation that rejects the Truth—finding the "right" words to pray can feel almost paralyzing.

When the disciples asked Jesus to teach them to pray, He instructed them to pray for God's will to be done (Luke 11:1–2 NKJV). So how can we know we are praying in accordance with the will of God? There's one sure way—*by praying God's Word back to Him*. When you don't know what to pray, open the Bible and ask God to do what He's promised to do or what He has revealed to be His will.

This resource will help you do just that. You'll find dozens of passages from Scripture to direct your prayers in various situations and seasons of life. Some of these passages are actual prayers that were recorded in the Scripture. Others weren't originally prayers but are nonetheless suitable to be prayed. These Scriptures will help you pray

FINDING THE WORDS TO PRAY

according to the will of God as it is found in His inspired Word. At the beginning of each section you'll also find words I've prayed through the years on the *Revive Our Hearts* daily program.

My hope is that this book will be a rich encouragement and will help you practice Scripture-based praying.

Praying with and for you,

Nancy

Nancy DeMoss Wolgemuth

Prayers for
SEASONS OF WAITING

Father, thank You for Your magnificent promises; for the certainty we have that the day will come when You return to make all things new. We know that the righteous will live by their faith. If we didn't have to wait for the outcome, we wouldn't need faith, and faith is what pleases You.

Teach us, Lord, to wait—to wait on You, to wait in confidence, to wait eagerly, to wait with patience, knowing that You do all things well and that You are fulfilling all Your purposes. Help us to keep our eyes on the end of the story, and in the meantime, to wait quietly for You.
I pray in Jesus' name, amen.

FINDING THE WORDS TO PRAY

Prayer One

Out of the depths I call to you, LORD!
Lord, listen to my voice;
let your ears be attentive
to my cry for help.

LORD, if you kept an account of iniquities,
Lord, who could stand?
But with you there is forgiveness,
so that you may be revered.

I wait for the LORD; I wait
and put my hope in his word.
I wait for the Lord
more than watchmen for the morning—
more than watchmen for the morning.

—Psalm 130:1–6

Dwell

What words or phrases stand out to you in this passage?

_____

_____

_____

_____

_____

Summarize the passage in a sentence or two.

_____

_____

_____

_____

_____

FINDING THE WORDS TO PRAY

Discover

What does this passage teach you about God?

_____

_____

_____

_____

_____

_____

What does this passage teach you about prayer?

_____

_____

_____

_____

_____

Pray

Using this passage as your guide, write out a prayer to the Lord.

_____

_____

_____

_____

_____

_____

_____

_____

Prayer Two

We wait for the LORD;
he is our help and shield.
For our hearts rejoice in him
because we trust in his holy name.
May your faithful love rest on us, LORD,
for we put our hope in you.

—Psalm 33:20–22

Dwell

What words or phrases stand out to you in this passage?

_____

_____

_____

_____

_____

Summarize the passage in a sentence or two.

_____

_____

_____

_____

_____

Discover

What does this passage teach you about God?

_____

_____

_____

_____

_____

What does this passage teach you about prayer?

_____

_____

_____

_____

_____

Pray

Using this passage as your guide, write out a prayer to the Lord.

_____

_____

_____

_____

_____

_____

_____

_____

Prayer Three

LORD—how long?
Turn and have compassion on your servants.
Satisfy us in the morning with your faithful love
so that we may shout with joy and be glad all
    our days.

—Psalm 90:13–14

Dwell

What words or phrases stand out to you in this passage?

Summarize the passage in a sentence or two.

Discover

What does this passage teach you about God?

_____

_____

_____

_____

_____

What does this passage teach you about prayer?

_____

_____

_____

_____

_____

PRAYERS FOR SEASONS OF WAITING

Pray

Using this passage as your guide, write out a prayer to the Lord.

_____

_____

_____

_____

_____

_____

_____

_____

Prayer Four

Rest in God alone, my soul,
for my hope comes from him.
He alone is my rock and my salvation,
my stronghold; I will not be shaken.
My salvation and glory depend on God,
    my strong rock.
My refuge is in God.
Trust in him at all times, you people;
pour out your hearts before him.
God is our refuge. *Selah*.

—Psalm 62:5–8

Dwell

What words or phrases stand out to you in this passage?

_____

_____

_____

_____

_____

Summarize the passage in a sentence or two.

_____

_____

_____

_____

_____

Discover

What does this passage teach you about God?

_____

_____

_____

_____

_____

What does this passage teach you about prayer?

_____

_____

_____

_____

_____

Pray

Using this passage as your guide, write out a prayer to the Lord.

_____

_____

_____

_____

_____

_____

_____

_____

FINDING THE WORDS TO PRAY

Prayer Five

I am certain that I will see the LORD's goodness
in the land of the living.
Wait for the LORD;
be strong, and let your heart be courageous.
Wait for the LORD.

—Psalm 27:13–14

Dwell

What words or phrases stand out to you in this passage?

_____

_____

_____

_____

_____

Summarize the passage in a sentence or two.

_____

_____

_____

_____

_____

Discover

What does this passage teach you about God?

_____

_____

_____

_____

_____

_____

What does this passage teach you about prayer?

_____

_____

_____

_____

_____

Pray

Using this passage as your guide, write out a prayer to the Lord.

_____

_____

_____

_____

_____

_____

_____

_____

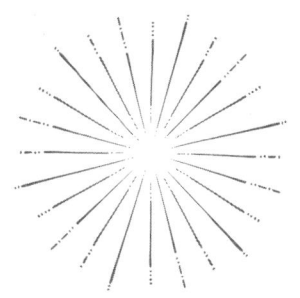

Prayers for WISDOM AND UNDERSTANDING

Lord, give us ears to hear and hearts to receive what You have said to us. Thank You that You're a God who has spoken, a God who has revealed Yourself. Thank You that Your Holy Spirit gives us direction, wisdom, and understanding. Help us to have quiet hearts, to be still long enough to listen to You and to Your Word. I pray in Jesus' name, amen.

: FINDING THE WORDS TO PRAY

Prayer Six

Now if any of you lacks wisdom, he should ask God—who gives to all generously and ungrudgingly—and it will be given to him.

—James 1:5

Dwell

What words or phrases stand out to you in this passage?

_____

_____

_____

_____

_____

Summarize the passage in a sentence or two.

_____

_____

_____

_____

_____

Discover

What does this passage teach you about God?

_____

_____

_____

_____

_____

_____

What does this passage teach you about prayer?

_____

_____

_____

_____

_____

Pray

Using this passage as your guide, write out a prayer to the Lord.

_____

_____

_____

_____

_____

_____

_____

_____

Prayer Seven

Lord, may you be blessed;
teach me your statutes.
With my lips I proclaim
all the judgments from your mouth.
I rejoice in the way revealed by your decrees
as much as in all riches.
I will meditate on your precepts
and think about your ways.
I will delight in your statutes;
I will not forget your word.

—Psalm 119:12–16

Dwell

What words or phrases stand out to you in this passage?

_____

_____

_____

_____

_____

Summarize the passage in a sentence or two.

_____

_____

_____

_____

_____

Discover

What does this passage teach you about God?

_____

_____

_____

_____

_____

What does this passage teach you about prayer?

_____

_____

_____

_____

_____

PRAYERS FOR WISDOM AND UNDERSTANDING

Pray

Using this passage as your guide, write out a prayer to the Lord.

_____

_____

_____

_____

_____

_____

_____

_____

Prayer Eight

Make your ways known to me, LORD;
teach me your paths.
Guide me in your truth and teach me,
for you are the God of my salvation;
I wait for you all day long.
Remember, LORD, your compassion
and your faithful love,
for they have existed from antiquity.

—Psalm 25:4–6

Dwell

What words or phrases stand out to you in this passage?

_____

_____

_____

_____

_____

Summarize the passage in a sentence or two.

_____

_____

_____

_____

_____

FINDING THE WORDS TO PRAY

Discover

What does this passage teach you about God?

_____

_____

_____

_____

_____

What does this passage teach you about prayer?

_____

_____

_____

_____

_____

PRAYERS FOR WISDOM AND UNDERSTANDING

Pray

Using this passage as your guide, write out a prayer to the Lord.

_____

_____

_____

_____

_____

_____

_____

_____

Prayer Nine

Help me understand your instruction,
and I will obey it
and follow it with all my heart.
Help me stay on the path of your commands,
for I take pleasure in it.

—Psalm 119:34–35

Dwell

What words or phrases stand out to you in this passage?

_____

_____

_____

_____

_____

Summarize the passage in a sentence or two.

_____

_____

_____

_____

_____

FINDING THE WORDS TO PRAY

Discover

What does this passage teach you about God?

_____

What does this passage teach you about prayer?

_____

PRAYERS FOR WISDOM AND UNDERSTANDING

Pray

Using this passage as your guide, write out a prayer to the Lord.

_____

_____

_____

_____

_____

_____

_____

_____

Prayer Ten

We haven't stopped praying for you. We are asking that you may be filled with the knowledge of his will in all wisdom and spiritual understanding, so that you may walk worthy of the Lord, fully pleasing to him: bearing fruit in every good work and growing in the knowledge of God, being strengthened with all power, according to his glorious might, so that you may have great endurance and patience, joyfully giving thanks to the Father, who has enabled you to share in the saints' inheritance in the light.

—Colossians 1:9–12

Dwell

What words or phrases stand out to you in this passage?

_____

_____

_____

_____

_____

Summarize the passage in a sentence or two.

_____

_____

_____

_____

_____

Discover

What does this passage teach you about God?

_____

_____

_____

_____

_____

_____

What does this passage teach you about prayer?

_____

_____

_____

_____

_____

Pray

Using this passage as your guide, write out a prayer to the Lord.

_____

_____

_____

_____

_____

_____

_____

_____

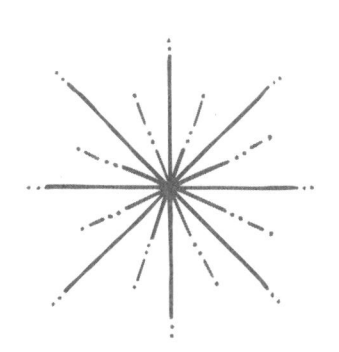

Prayers for TRANSFORMATION

Oh Lord, we pray that You would do a sweet work of gospel grace in each of our hearts—not to put us under a burden of more things to do but to show us the delight, the joy, that can be had—the freedom, fullness, and fruitfulness—as a result of learning to live out the beauty of the gospel together, so that in everything we may adorn the doctrine of God our Savior. And we pray it in Jesus' sweet name, amen.

FINDING THE WORDS TO PRAY

Prayer Eleven

LORD, set up a guard for my mouth;
keep watch at the door of my lips.
Do not let my heart turn to any evil thing
or perform wicked acts with evildoers.
Do not let me feast on their delicacies.

—Psalm 141:3–4

Dwell

What words or phrases stand out to you in this passage?

Summarize the passage in a sentence or two.

Discover

What does this passage teach you about God?

_____

_____

_____

_____

_____

What does this passage teach you about prayer?

_____

_____

_____

_____

Pray

Using this passage as your guide, write out a prayer to the Lord.

_____

_____

_____

_____

_____

_____

_____

_____

Prayer Twelve

May the words of my mouth
and the meditation of my heart
be acceptable to you,
LORD, my rock and my Redeemer.

—Psalm 19:14

Dwell

What words or phrases stand out to you in this passage?

_____

_____

_____

_____

_____

Summarize the passage in a sentence or two.

_____

_____

_____

_____

_____

FINDING THE WORDS TO PRAY

Discover

What does this passage teach you about God?

_____

_____

_____

_____

_____

What does this passage teach you about prayer?

_____

_____

_____

_____

_____

Pray

Using this passage as your guide, write out a prayer to the Lord.

Prayer Thirteen

Teach me, LORD, the meaning of your statutes,
and I will always keep them.
Help me understand your instruction,
and I will obey it
and follow it with all my heart.
Help me stay on the path of your commands,
for I take pleasure in it.
Turn my heart to your decrees
and not to dishonest profit.
Turn my eyes
from looking at what is worthless;
give me life in your ways.

—Psalm 119:33–37

Dwell

What words or phrases stand out to you in this passage?

_____

_____

_____

_____

_____

Summarize the passage in a sentence or two.

_____

_____

_____

_____

_____

Discover

What does this passage teach you about God?

_____

_____

_____

_____

_____

What does this passage teach you about prayer?

_____

_____

_____

_____

_____

PRAYERS FOR TRANSFORMATION

Pray

Using this passage as your guide, write out a prayer to the Lord.

Prayer Fourteen

Search me, God, and know my heart;
test me and know my concerns.
See if there is any offensive way in me;
lead me in the everlasting way.

—Psalm 139:23–24

PRAYERS FOR TRANSFORMATION

Dwell

What words or phrases stand out to you in this passage?

_____

_____

_____

_____

_____

Summarize the passage in a sentence or two.

_____

_____

_____

_____

_____

Discover

What does this passage teach you about God?

What does this passage teach you about prayer?

Pray

Using this passage as your guide, write out a prayer to the Lord.

_____

_____

_____

_____

_____

_____

_____

_____

Prayer Fifteen

We always pray for you that our God will make you worthy of his calling, and by his power fulfill your every desire to do good and your work produced by faith, so that the name of our Lord Jesus will be glorified by you, and you by him, according to the grace of our God and the Lord Jesus Christ.

—2 Thessalonians 1:11–12

Dwell

What words or phrases stand out to you in this passage?

_____

_____

_____

_____

_____

Summarize the passage in a sentence or two.

_____

_____

_____

_____

_____

FINDING THE WORDS TO PRAY

Discover

What does this passage teach you about God?

_____

_____

_____

_____

_____

_____

What does this passage teach you about prayer?

_____

_____

_____

_____

_____

Pray

Using this passage as your guide, write out a prayer to the Lord.

_____

_____

_____

_____

_____

_____

_____

_____

Prayer Sixteen

> Let us hold on to the confession of our hope without wavering, since he who promised is faithful. And let us consider one another in order to provoke love and good works, not neglecting to gather together, as some are in the habit of doing, but encouraging each other, and all the more as you see the day approaching.
>
> —Hebrews 10:23–25

Dwell

What words or phrases stand out to you in this passage?

___

Summarize the passage in a sentence or two.

___

Discover

What does this passage teach you about God?

_____

_____

_____

_____

_____

What does this passage teach you about prayer?

_____

_____

_____

_____

_____

Pray

Using this passage as your guide, write out a prayer to the Lord.

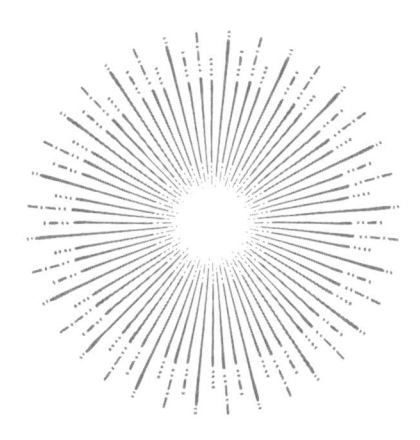

Prayers for
THE CHURCH

Lord, thank You for the wonder of Your plan for the Church. Thank You for this great mystery that You have made known to us. Thank You for the privilege of being a part of the Body of Christ. We're part of each other. We're united with Christ; we're united with one another. We need each other. Help us to nourish and cherish and care for the Body as You do, for we are members of Your Body and members of one another.
I pray in Jesus' name, amen.

FINDING THE WORDS TO PRAY

Prayer Seventeen

I pray this: that your love will keep on growing in knowledge and every kind of discernment, so that you may approve the things that are superior and may be pure and blameless in the day of Christ, filled with the fruit of righteousness that comes through Jesus Christ to the glory and praise of God.

—Philippians 1:9–11

Dwell

What words or phrases stand out to you in this passage?

Summarize the passage in a sentence or two.

FINDING THE WORDS TO PRAY

Discover

What does this passage teach you about God?

_____

_____

_____

_____

_____

_____

What does this passage teach you about prayer?

_____

_____

_____

_____

_____

PRAYERS FOR THE CHURCH

Pray

Using this passage as your guide, write out a prayer to the Lord.

Prayer Eighteen

Now may the God of peace, who brought up from the dead our Lord Jesus—the great Shepherd of the sheep—through the blood of the everlasting covenant, equip you with everything good to do his will, working in us what is pleasing in his sight, through Jesus Christ, to whom be glory forever and ever. Amen.

—Hebrews 13:20–21

Dwell

What words or phrases stand out to you in this passage?

_____

_____

_____

_____

_____

Summarize the passage in a sentence or two.

_____

_____

_____

_____

_____

Discover

What does this passage teach you about God?

_____

_____

_____

_____

_____

What does this passage teach you about prayer?

_____

_____

_____

_____

_____

PRAYERS FOR THE CHURCH

Pray

Using this passage as your guide, write out a prayer to the Lord.

_____

_____

_____

_____

_____

_____

_____

_____

Prayer Nineteen

They devoted themselves to the apostles' teaching, to the fellowship, to the breaking of bread, and to prayer. Everyone was filled with awe, and many wonders and signs were being performed through the apostles. Now all the believers were together and held all things in common. They sold their possessions and property and distributed the proceeds to all, as any had need. Every day they devoted themselves to meeting together in the temple, and broke bread from house to house. They ate their food with joyful and sincere hearts, praising God and enjoying the favor of all the people. Every day the Lord added to their number those who were being saved.

—Acts 2:42–47

Dwell

What words or phrases stand out to you in this passage?

Summarize the passage in a sentence or two.

Discover

What does this passage teach you about God?

What does this passage teach you about prayer?

PRAYERS FOR THE CHURCH

Pray

Using this passage as your guide, write out a prayer to the Lord.

Prayer Twenty

Therefore I, the prisoner in the Lord, urge you to walk worthy of the calling you have received, with all humility and gentleness, with patience, bearing with one another in love, making every effort to keep the unity of the Spirit through the bond of peace. There is one body and one Spirit—just as you were called to one hope at your calling—one Lord, one faith, one baptism, one God and Father of all, who is above all and through all and in all.

—Ephesians 4:1–6

Dwell

What words or phrases stand out to you in this passage?

Summarize the passage in a sentence or two.

Discover

What does this passage teach you about God?

What does this passage teach you about prayer?

PRAYERS FOR THE CHURCH

Pray

Using this passage as your guide, write out a prayer to the Lord.

Prayers for PRODIGALS

Lord, so many we know are hurting deeply
because of estranged family relationships.
Hearts have been wounded by prodigal children,
parents, mates, and siblings who are far from
the Father and far from home. Please minister
tailor-made hope and peace to broken hearts and
homes. You are a redeeming God who restores
and heals. In Your mercy, may prodigals be drawn
back first to You and then to their families.
We pray in Jesus' name, amen.

FINDING THE WORDS TO PRAY

Prayer Twenty-One

Where can I go to escape your Spirit?
Where can I flee from your presence?
If I go up to heaven, you are there;
if I make my bed in Sheol, you are there.
If I fly on the wings of the dawn
and settle down on the western horizon,
even there your hand will lead me;
your right hand will hold on to me.
If I say, "Surely the darkness will hide me,
and the light around me will be night"—
even the darkness is not dark to you.
The night shines like the day;
darkness and light are alike to you.

—Psalm 139:7–12

Dwell

What words or phrases stand out to you in this passage?

_____

_____

_____

_____

_____

Summarize the passage in a sentence or two.

_____

_____

_____

_____

_____

Discover

What does this passage teach you about God?

What does this passage teach you about prayer?

Pray

Using this passage as your guide, write out a prayer to the Lord.

_____

_____

_____

_____

_____

_____

_____

_____

Prayer Twenty-Two

I pray that the God of our Lord Jesus Christ, the glorious Father, would give you the Spirit of wisdom and revelation in the knowledge of him. I pray that the eyes of your heart may be enlightened so that you may know what is the hope of his calling, what is the wealth of his glorious inheritance in the saints, and what is the immeasurable greatness of his power toward us who believe, according to the mighty working of his strength.

—Ephesians 1:17–19

Dwell

What words or phrases stand out to you in this passage?

_____

_____

_____

_____

_____

Summarize the passage in a sentence or two.

_____

_____

_____

_____

_____

Discover

What does this passage teach you about God?

What does this passage teach you about prayer?

PRAYERS FOR PRODIGALS

Pray

Using this passage as your guide, write out a prayer to the Lord.

FINDING THE WORDS TO PRAY

Prayer Twenty-Three

> I am sure of this, that he who started a good work in you will carry it on to completion until the day of Christ Jesus.
>
> —Philippians 1:6

Dwell

What words or phrases stand out to you in this passage?

_____

_____

_____

_____

_____

Summarize the passage in a sentence or two.

_____

_____

_____

_____

_____

Discover

What does this passage teach you about God?

What does this passage teach you about prayer?

Pray

Using this passage as your guide, write out a prayer to the Lord.

_____

_____

_____

_____

_____

_____

_____

_____

Prayer Twenty-Four

> For I am persuaded that neither death nor life, nor angels nor rulers, nor things present nor things to come, nor powers, nor height nor depth, nor any other created thing will be able to separate us from the love of God that is in Christ Jesus our Lord.
>
> —Romans 8:38–39

Dwell

What words or phrases stand out to you in this passage?

_____

_____

_____

_____

_____

Summarize the passage in a sentence or two.

_____

_____

_____

_____

_____

Discover

What does this passage teach you about God?

_____

_____

_____

_____

_____

_____

What does this passage teach you about prayer?

_____

_____

_____

_____

_____

PRAYERS FOR PRODIGALS

Pray

Using this passage as your guide, write out a prayer to the Lord.

Prayer Twenty-Five

"But while the son was still a long way off, his father saw him and was filled with compassion. He ran, threw his arms around his neck, and kissed him. The son said to him, 'Father, I have sinned against heaven and in your sight. I'm no longer worthy to be called your son.'

"But the father told his servants, 'Quick! Bring out the best robe and put it on him; put a ring on his finger and sandals on his feet. Then bring the fattened calf and slaughter it, and let's celebrate with a feast, because this son of mine was dead and is alive again; he was lost and is found!' So they began to celebrate."

—Luke 15:20–24

Dwell

What words or phrases stand out to you in this passage?

_____

_____

_____

_____

_____

Summarize the passage in a sentence or two.

_____

_____

_____

_____

_____

Discover

What does this passage teach you about God?

What does this passage teach you about prayer?

Pray

Using this passage as your guide, write out a prayer to the Lord.

_____

_____

_____

_____

_____

_____

_____

_____

Prayers for COMFORT

Oh Lord, would You comfort us with the comfort of the gospel? And would You save us from looking anywhere else for hope other than to Christ, and Christ alone? In Him is all our hope, all our comfort in life and in death, and for that, we give You thanks. We celebrate for our debt of sin has been paid and we've been set free, delivered, from the tyranny of Satan! In Jesus' name, amen.

FINDING THE WORDS TO PRAY

Prayer Twenty-Six

Even when I go through the darkest valley,
I fear no danger,
for you are with me;
your rod and your staff—they comfort me.

You prepare a table before me
in the presence of my enemies;
you anoint my head with oil;
my cup overflows.
Only goodness and faithful love will pursue me
all the days of my life,
and I will dwell in the house of the LORD
as long as I live.

—Psalm 23:4–6

Dwell

What words or phrases stand out to you in this passage?

Summarize the passage in a sentence or two.

Discover

What does this passage teach you about God?

_____

_____

_____

_____

_____

What does this passage teach you about prayer?

_____

_____

_____

_____

_____

Pray

Using this passage as your guide, write out a prayer to the Lord.

_____

_____

_____

_____

_____

_____

_____

Prayer Twenty-Seven

When I am afraid,
I will trust in you.
In God, whose word I praise,
in God I trust; I will not be afraid.
What can mere mortals do to me?

—Psalm 56:3–4

Dwell

What words or phrases stand out to you in this passage?

_____

_____

_____

_____

_____

Summarize the passage in a sentence or two.

_____

_____

_____

_____

_____

Discover

What does this passage teach you about God?

What does this passage teach you about prayer?

Pray

Using this passage as your guide, write out a prayer to the Lord.

_____

_____

_____

_____

_____

_____

_____

_____

FINDING THE WORDS TO PRAY

Prayer Twenty-Eight

> If I say, "My foot is slipping,"
> your faithful love will support me, LORD.
> When I am filled with cares,
> your comfort brings me joy.
>
> —Psalm 94:18–19

Dwell

What words or phrases stand out to you in this passage?

Summarize the passage in a sentence or two.

FINDING THE WORDS TO PRAY

Discover

What does this passage teach you about God?

_____

_____

_____

_____

_____

_____

What does this passage teach you about prayer?

_____

_____

_____

_____

_____

Pray

Using this passage as your guide, write out a prayer to the Lord.

FINDING THE WORDS TO PRAY

Prayer Twenty-Nine

> I will bless the LORD who counsels me—
> even at night when my thoughts trouble me.
> I always let the LORD guide me.
> Because he is at my right hand,
> I will not be shaken.
>
> —Psalm 16:7–8

Dwell

What words or phrases stand out to you in this passage?

_____

_____

_____

_____

_____

Summarize the passage in a sentence or two.

_____

_____

_____

_____

_____

Discover

What does this passage teach you about God?

_____

_____

_____

_____

_____

_____

What does this passage teach you about prayer?

_____

_____

_____

_____

_____

Pray

Using this passage as your guide, write out a prayer to the Lord.

_____

_____

_____

_____

_____

_____

_____

_____

FINDING THE WORDS TO PRAY

Prayer Thirty

> Yet I call this to mind,
> and therefore I have hope:
>
> Because of the LORD's faithful love
> we do not perish,
> for his mercies never end.
> They are new every morning;
> great is your faithfulness!
> I say, "The LORD is my portion,
> therefore I will put my hope in him."
>
> —Lamentations 3:21–24

Dwell

What words or phrases stand out to you in this passage?

_____

_____

_____

_____

_____

Summarize the passage in a sentence or two.

_____

_____

_____

_____

_____

Discover

What does this passage teach you about God?

_____

_____

_____

_____

_____

_____

What does this passage teach you about prayer?

_____

_____

_____

_____

_____

Pray

Using this passage as your guide, write out a prayer to the Lord.

_____

_____

_____

_____

_____

_____

_____

_____

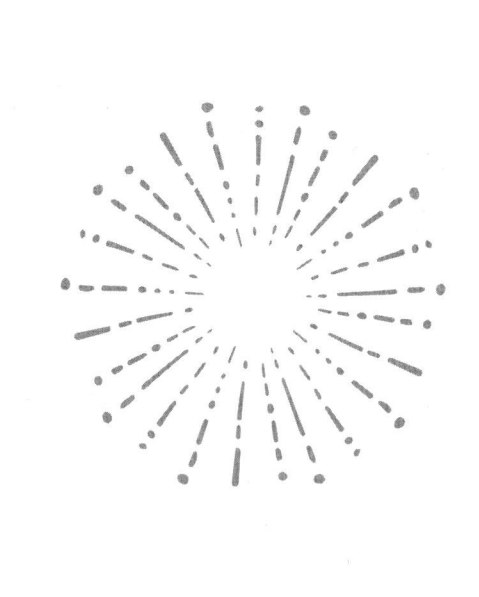

Prayers of DESPERATION

Lord, life is hard. Life hurts. There is sorrow.
There is death. The whole creation groans and
travails in pain. And yet we have this hope that
You are the God of our salvation and that
You are making all things new.

We affirm that You are good, that You are fulfilling
Your eternal purposes, and that one day there will
be no more sorrow, pain, tears, or dying.

And Lord, if affliction helps prepare us for that
day, then may we embrace it with joy and faith.
We pray in Jesus' name, amen.

FINDING THE WORDS TO PRAY

Prayer Thirty-One

"I do believe; help my unbelief!"

—Mark 9:24

Dwell

What words or phrases stand out to you in this passage?

_____

_____

_____

_____

_____

Summarize the passage in a sentence or two.

_____

_____

_____

_____

_____

Discover

What does this passage teach you about God?

_____

_____

_____

_____

_____

_____

What does this passage teach you about prayer?

_____

_____

_____

_____

_____

Pray

Using this passage as your guide, write out a prayer to the Lord.

FINDING THE WORDS TO PRAY

Prayer Thirty-Two

Why, my soul, are you so dejected?
Why are you in such turmoil?
Put your hope in God, for I will still praise him,
my Savior and my God.

—Psalm 42:11

Dwell

What words or phrases stand out to you in this passage?

Summarize the passage in a sentence or two.

FINDING THE WORDS TO PRAY

Discover

What does this passage teach you about God?

_____

_____

_____

_____

_____

_____

What does this passage teach you about prayer?

_____

_____

_____

_____

_____

Pray

Using this passage as your guide, write out a prayer to the Lord.

_____

_____

_____

_____

_____

_____

_____

_____

FINDING THE WORDS TO PRAY

Prayer Thirty-Three

> Turn to me and be gracious to me,
> for I am alone and afflicted.
> The distresses of my heart increase;
> bring me out of my sufferings.
>
> —Psalm 25:16–17

Dwell

What words or phrases stand out to you in this passage?

_____

_____

_____

_____

_____

Summarize the passage in a sentence or two.

_____

_____

_____

_____

_____

Discover

What does this passage teach you about God?

What does this passage teach you about prayer?

Pray

Using this passage as your guide, write out a prayer to the Lord.

_____

_____

_____

_____

_____

_____

_____

_____

Prayer Thirty-Four

My God, my God, why have you abandoned me?
Why are you so far from my deliverance
and from my words of groaning?
My God, I cry by day, but you do not answer,
by night, yet I have no rest.
But you are holy,
enthroned on the praises of Israel.
Our ancestors trusted in you;
they trusted, and you rescued them.
They cried to you and were set free;
they trusted in you and were not disgraced.

—Psalm 22:1–5

Dwell

What words or phrases stand out to you in this passage?

_____

_____

_____

_____

_____

Summarize the passage in a sentence or two.

_____

_____

_____

_____

_____

Discover

What does this passage teach you about God?

_____

_____

_____

_____

_____

_____

What does this passage teach you about prayer?

_____

_____

_____

_____

_____

Pray

Using this passage as your guide, write out a prayer to the Lord.

_____

_____

_____

_____

_____

_____

_____

_____

FINDING THE WORDS TO PRAY

Prayer Thirty-Five

God, hear my cry;
pay attention to my prayer.
I call to you from the ends of the earth
when my heart is without strength.
Lead me to a rock that is high above me,
for you have been a refuge for me,
a strong tower in the face of the enemy.
I will dwell in your tent forever
and take refuge under the shelter of your wings. *Selah*.

—Psalm 61:1–4

Dwell

What words or phrases stand out to you in this passage?

_____

_____

_____

_____

_____

Summarize the passage in a sentence or two.

_____

_____

_____

_____

_____

Discover

What does this passage teach you about God?

_____

_____

_____

_____

_____

_____

What does this passage teach you about prayer?

_____

_____

_____

_____

_____

Pray

Using this passage as your guide, write out a prayer to the Lord.

_____

_____

_____

_____

_____

_____

_____

_____

Prayers of REPENTANCE

Father, how we thank You for Calvary, for the cross, for Jesus. We thank You for the blood that was shed for our sins; for our pardon, peace, reconciliation, atonement, and redemption; and that we might receive forgiveness full and free.

Oh, Father, I pray that the message of the cross, the gospel, the good news of Jesus Christ would grip and ravish our hearts, that we'd be overcome and overjoyed with the wonder of what Christ has done for us. May guilty sinners, as we all are, find relief and release and pardon at the cross of Christ this day. Oh God, our Father, forgive us our debts for Jesus' sake and in His name, amen.

FINDING THE WORDS TO PRAY

Prayer Thirty-Six

Be gracious to me, God,
according to your faithful love;
according to your abundant compassion,
blot out my rebellion.
Completely wash away my guilt
and cleanse me from my sin.
For I am conscious of my rebellion,
and my sin is always before me.
Against you—you alone—I have sinned
and done this evil in your sight.
So you are right when you pass sentence;
you are blameless when you judge.
Indeed, I was guilty when I was born;
I was sinful when my mother conceived me.

Surely you desire integrity in the inner self,
and you teach me wisdom deep within.
Purify me with hyssop, and I will be clean;
wash me, and I will be whiter than snow.
Let me hear joy and gladness;
let the bones you have crushed rejoice.
Turn your face away from my sins
and blot out all my guilt.

God, create a clean heart for me
and renew a steadfast spirit within me.
Do not banish me from your presence
or take your Holy Spirit from me.
Restore the joy of your salvation to me,
and sustain me by giving me a willing spirit.
Then I will teach the rebellious your ways,
and sinners will return to you.

FINDING THE WORDS TO PRAY

> Save me from the guilt of bloodshed, God—
> God of my salvation—
> and my tongue will sing of your righteousness.
> Lord, open my lips,
> and my mouth will declare your praise.
> You do not want a sacrifice, or I would give it;
> you are not pleased with a burnt offering.
> The sacrifice pleasing to God is a broken spirit.
> You will not despise a broken and humbled heart, God.
>
> —Psalm 51:1–17

PRAYERS OF REPENTANCE

Dwell

What words or phrases stand out to you in this passage?

_____

_____

_____

_____

_____

Summarize the passage in a sentence or two.

_____

_____

_____

_____

_____

Discover

What does this passage teach you about God?

What does this passage teach you about prayer?

PRAYERS OF REPENTANCE

Pray

Using this passage as your guide, write out a prayer to the Lord.

FINDING THE WORDS TO PRAY

Prayer Thirty-Seven

> Who is a God like you,
> forgiving iniquity and passing over rebellion
> for the remnant of his inheritance?
> He does not hold on to his anger forever
> because he delights in faithful love.
> He will again have compassion on us;
> he will vanquish our iniquities.
> You will cast all our sins
> into the depths of the sea.
>
> —Micah 7:18–19

PRAYERS OF REPENTANCE

Dwell

What words or phrases stand out to you in this passage?

Summarize the passage in a sentence or two.

FINDING THE WORDS TO PRAY

Discover

What does this passage teach you about God?

_____

_____

_____

_____

_____

_____

What does this passage teach you about prayer?

_____

_____

_____

_____

_____

Pray

Using this passage as your guide, write out a prayer to the Lord.

_____

_____

_____

_____

_____

_____

_____

_____

FINDING THE WORDS TO PRAY

Prayer Thirty-Eight

"God, have mercy on me, a sinner!"

—Luke 18:13

Dwell

What words or phrases stand out to you in this passage?

___

___

___

___

___

Summarize the passage in a sentence or two.

___

___

___

___

___

FINDING THE WORDS TO PRAY

Discover

What does this passage teach you about God?

_____

_____

_____

_____

_____

What does this passage teach you about prayer?

_____

_____

_____

_____

_____

PRAYERS OF REPENTANCE

Pray

Using this passage as your guide, write out a prayer to the Lord.

Prayer Thirty-Nine

How joyful is the one
whose transgression is forgiven,
whose sin is covered!
How joyful is a person whom
the LORD does not charge with iniquity
and in whose spirit is no deceit!

When I kept silent, my bones became brittle
from my groaning all day long.
For day and night your hand was heavy on me;
my strength was drained
as in the summer's heat. *Selah.*

PRAYERS OF REPENTANCE

Then I acknowledged my sin to you
and did not conceal my iniquity.
I said, "I will confess my transgressions to the LORD,"
and you forgave the guilt of my sin. *Selah*.

—Psalm 32:1–5

Dwell

What words or phrases stand out to you in this passage?

_____

_____

_____

_____

_____

Summarize the passage in a sentence or two.

_____

_____

_____

_____

_____

Discover

What does this passage teach you about God?

_____

_____

_____

_____

_____

_____

What does this passage teach you about prayer?

_____

_____

_____

_____

_____

FINDING THE WORDS TO PRAY

Pray

Using this passage as your guide, write out a prayer to the Lord.

_____
_____
_____
_____
_____
_____
_____
_____
_____
_____
_____

PRAYERS OF REPENTANCE

Prayer Forty

> If we say, "We have no sin," we are deceiving ourselves, and the truth is not in us. If we confess our sins, he is faithful and righteous to forgive us our sins and to cleanse us from all unrighteousness. If we say, "We have not sinned," we make him a liar, and his word is not in us.
>
> —1 John 1:8–10

Dwell

What words or phrases stand out to you in this passage?

_____

_____

_____

_____

_____

Summarize the passage in a sentence or two.

_____

_____

_____

_____

_____

Discover

What does this passage teach you about God?

What does this passage teach you about prayer?

PRAYERS OF REPENTANCE

Pray

Using this passage as your guide, write out a prayer to the Lord.

_____

_____

_____

_____

_____

_____

_____

_____

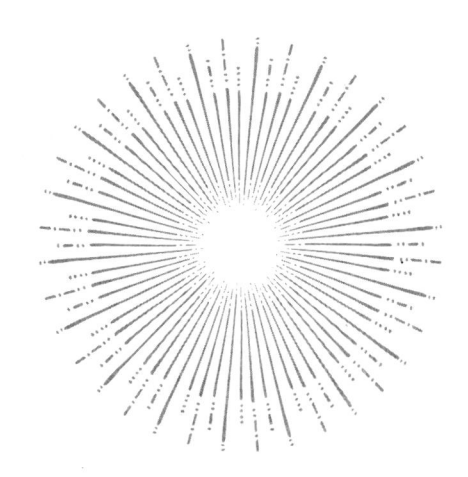

Prayers for
REVIVAL

Lord, have mercy on us, Your people, for we have sinned. We desperately need Your mercy. Restore, renew, and revive for Jesus' sake we pray, amen.

Prayer Forty-One

Ah, Lord—the great and awe-inspiring God who keeps his gracious covenant with those who love him and keep his commands—we have sinned, done wrong, acted wickedly, rebelled, and turned away from your commands and ordinances. We have not listened to your servants the prophets, who spoke in your name to our kings, leaders, ancestors, and all the people of the land....

Compassion and forgiveness belong to the Lord our God, though we have rebelled against him and have not obeyed the LORD our God by following his instructions that he set before us through his servants the prophets....

Listen closely, my God, and hear. Open your eyes and see our desolations and the city that bears your name. For we are not presenting our petitions before you based on our righteous acts, but based on your abundant compassion. Lord, hear! Lord, forgive! Lord, listen and act! My God, for your own sake, do not delay, because your city and your people bear your name.

— Daniel 9:4–6; 9–10; 18–19

Dwell

What words or phrases stand out to you in this passage?

_____

_____

_____

_____

_____

Summarize the passage in a sentence or two.

_____

_____

_____

_____

_____

Discover

What does this passage teach you about God?

What does this passage teach you about prayer?

FINDING THE WORDS TO PRAY

Pray

Using this passage as your guide, write out a prayer to the Lord.

PRAYERS FOR REVIVAL

FINDING THE WORDS TO PRAY

Prayer Forty-Two

Return to us, God of our salvation,
and abandon your displeasure with us.
Will you be angry with us forever?
Will you prolong your anger for all generations?
Will you not revive us again
so that your people may rejoice in you?
Show us your faithful love, LORD,
and give us your salvation.

—Psalm 85:4–7

Dwell

What words or phrases stand out to you in this passage?

_____

_____

_____

_____

_____

Summarize the passage in a sentence or two.

_____

_____

_____

_____

_____

Discover

What does this passage teach you about God?

_____

_____

_____

_____

_____

What does this passage teach you about prayer?

_____

_____

_____

_____

_____

Pray

Using this passage as your guide, write out a prayer to the Lord.

_____

_____

_____

_____

_____

_____

_____

_____

Prayer Forty-Three

Therefore, submit to God. Resist the devil, and he will flee from you. Draw near to God, and he will draw near to you. Cleanse your hands, sinners, and purify your hearts, you double-minded. Be miserable and mourn and weep. Let your laughter be turned to mourning and your joy to gloom. Humble yourselves before the Lord, and he will exalt you.

—James 4:7–10

Dwell

What words or phrases stand out to you in this passage?

_____

_____

_____

_____

_____

Summarize the passage in a sentence or two.

_____

_____

_____

_____

_____

Discover

What does this passage teach you about God?

_____

_____

_____

_____

_____

_____

What does this passage teach you about prayer?

_____

_____

_____

_____

_____

PRAYERS FOR REVIVAL

Pray

Using this passage as your guide, write out a prayer to the Lord.

FINDING THE WORDS TO PRAY

Prayer Forty-Four

> LORD, I have heard the report about you;
> LORD, I stand in awe of your deeds.
> Revive your work in these years;
> make it known in these years.
> In your wrath remember mercy!
>
> —Habakkuk 3:2

PRAYERS FOR REVIVAL

Dwell

What words or phrases stand out to you in this passage?

_____

_____

_____

_____

_____

Summarize the passage in a sentence or two.

_____

_____

_____

_____

_____

Discover

What does this passage teach you about God?

_____

_____

_____

_____

_____

_____

What does this passage teach you about prayer?

_____

_____

_____

_____

_____

PRAYERS FOR REVIVAL

Pray

Using this passage as your guide, write out a prayer to the Lord.

_____

_____

_____

_____

_____

_____

_____

_____

Prayer Forty-Five

> Restore us, God of Armies;
> make your face shine on us, so that we may be saved.
>
> —Psalm 80:7

Dwell

What words or phrases stand out to you in this passage?

_____

_____

_____

_____

_____

Summarize the passage in a sentence or two.

_____

_____

_____

_____

_____

Discover

What does this passage teach you about God?

_____

_____

_____

_____

_____

_____

What does this passage teach you about prayer?

_____

_____

_____

_____

_____

Pray

Using this passage as your guide, write out a prayer to the Lord.

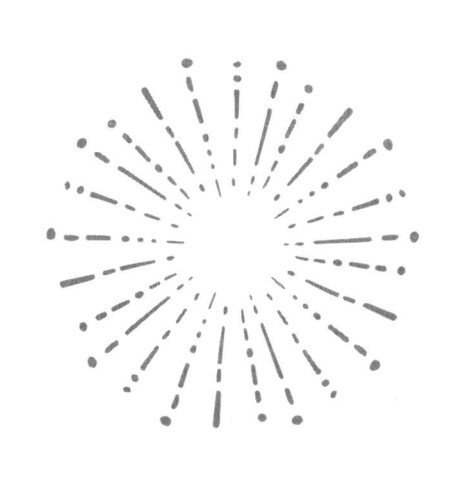

Prayers of PRAISE

Oh Lord, we want to seek Your glory, Your kingdom, and Your will. You are worthy of praise. You are our Father in heaven. Your name is holy. We lift You up. We exalt You.

May the things that are uppermost on Your heart be uppermost on our hearts. Teach us praise before petition and You before us. May it be Your kingdom, not ours; Your will, not ours; Your name, not ours that we seek above all else. We pray in Jesus' name, amen.

FINDING THE WORDS TO PRAY

Prayer Forty-Six

I will exalt you, LORD,
because you have lifted me up
and have not allowed my enemies
to triumph over me.
LORD my God,
I cried to you for help, and you healed me.
LORD, you brought me up from Sheol;
you spared me from among those
going down to the Pit.

Sing to the LORD, you his faithful ones,
and praise his holy name.
For his anger lasts only a moment,

but his favor, a lifetime.
Weeping may stay overnight,
but there is joy in the morning.

When I was secure, I said,
"I will never be shaken."
LORD, when you showed your favor,
you made me stand like a strong mountain;
when you hid your face, I was terrified.
LORD, I called to you;
I sought favor from my Lord:
"What gain is there in my death,
if I go down to the Pit?
Will the dust praise you?
Will it proclaim your truth?
LORD, listen and be gracious to me;
LORD, be my helper."

You turned my lament into dancing;
you removed my sackcloth
and clothed me with gladness,
so that I can sing to you and not be silent.
LORD my God, I will praise you forever.

—Psalm 30

Dwell

What words or phrases stand out to you in this passage?

_____

_____

_____

_____

_____

Summarize the passage in a sentence or two.

_____

_____

_____

_____

_____

Discover

What does this passage teach you about God?

What does this passage teach you about prayer?

Pray

Using this passage as your guide, write out a prayer to the Lord.

Prayer Forty-Seven

My soul, bless the LORD,
and all that is within me, bless his holy name.
My soul, bless the LORD,
and do not forget all his benefits.

He forgives all your iniquity;
he heals all your diseases.
He redeems your life from the Pit;
he crowns you with faithful love and compassion.
He satisfies you with good things;
your youth is renewed like the eagle.

The LORD executes acts of righteousness
and justice for all the oppressed.
He revealed his ways to Moses,
his deeds to the people of Israel.
The LORD is compassionate and gracious,
slow to anger and abounding in faithful love.
He will not always accuse us
or be angry forever.
He has not dealt with us as our sins deserve
or repaid us according to our iniquities.

For as high as the heavens are above the earth,
so great is his faithful love
toward those who fear him.
As far as the east is from the west,
so far has he removed
our transgressions from us.

FINDING THE WORDS TO PRAY

As a father has compassion on his children,
so the LORD has compassion on those who fear him.
For he knows what we are made of,
remembering that we are dust.

—Psalm 103:1–14

Dwell

What words or phrases stand out to you in this passage?

_____

_____

_____

_____

_____

Summarize the passage in a sentence or two.

_____

_____

_____

_____

_____

FINDING THE WORDS TO PRAY

Discover

What does this passage teach you about God?

What does this passage teach you about prayer?

Pray

Using this passage as your guide, write out a prayer to the Lord.

_____

_____

_____

_____

_____

_____

_____

_____

FINDING THE WORDS TO PRAY

Prayer Forty-Eight

> LORD, you are my God;
> I will exalt you. I will praise your name,
> for you have accomplished wonders,
> plans formed long ago, with perfect faithfulness.
>
> —Isaiah 25:1

Dwell

What words or phrases stand out to you in this passage?

Summarize the passage in a sentence or two.

FINDING THE WORDS TO PRAY

Discover

What does this passage teach you about God?

_____

_____

_____

_____

_____

_____

What does this passage teach you about prayer?

_____

_____

_____

_____

_____

Pray

Using this passage as your guide, write out a prayer to the Lord.

_____

_____

_____

_____

_____

_____

_____

_____

Prayer Forty-Nine

> I will praise you, Lord, among the peoples;
> I will sing praises to you among the nations.
> For your faithful love is as high as the heavens;
> your faithfulness reaches the clouds.
> God, be exalted above the heavens;
> let your glory be over the whole earth.
>
> —Psalm 57:9–11

Dwell

What words or phrases stand out to you in this passage?

_____

_____

_____

_____

_____

Summarize the passage in a sentence or two.

_____

_____

_____

_____

_____

Discover

What does this passage teach you about God?

_____

_____

_____

_____

_____

_____

What does this passage teach you about prayer?

_____

_____

_____

_____

_____

PRAYERS OF PRAISE

Pray

Using this passage as your guide, write out a prayer to the Lord.

_____

_____

_____

_____

_____

_____

_____

_____

Prayer Fifty

May you be blessed, LORD God of our father Israel, from eternity to eternity. Yours, LORD, is the greatness and the power and the glory and the splendor and the majesty, for everything in the heavens and on earth belongs to you. Yours, LORD, is the kingdom, and you are exalted as head over all. Riches and honor come from you, and you are the ruler of everything. Power and might are in your hand, and it is in your hand to make great and to give strength to all. Now therefore, our God, we give you thanks and praise your glorious name.

—1 Chronicles 29:10–13

Dwell

What words or phrases stand out to you in this passage?

_____

_____

_____

_____

_____

Summarize the passage in a sentence or two.

_____

_____

_____

_____

_____

FINDING THE WORDS TO PRAY

Discover

What does this passage teach you about God?

_____

_____

_____

_____

_____

What does this passage teach you about prayer?

_____

_____

_____

_____

_____

PRAYERS OF PRAISE

Pray

Using this passage as your guide, write out a prayer to the Lord.